MW00678789

JUICES &
HEALTH DRINKS

Written and compiled by Catherine Larner
Photography by Top That! and Banana Stock

TOP THAT!™

Copyright © 2004 Top That! Publishing plc
Top That! Publishing,
25031 W. Avenue Stanford,
Suite #60, Valencia
CA 91355
All rights reserved
www.topthatpublishing.com

CONTENTS

3

WHY JUICE?

Juices are quick to make, taste great and are packed with goodness—an ideal boost for busy lives

Fresh fruit and vegetables are the best possible foods. The vitamins and minerals they contain help keep our skin clear, our hair shiny, bring a glow to our cheeks, and get rid of many of the toxins of modern living.

The raw juice delivers all that goodness literally in an instant, with no waste and no munching. By making your own juice, you can combine flavors and ensure the purest ingredients. So, what's stopping you? Juices are cleansing, healing, energizing, and... delicious!

SMOOTH AWAY

Add fiber or protein to your drinks through making fruit and vegetable smoothies

You don't have to use a juicer to make some great drinks. By mixing whole ingredients into a pulp in a blender, you can create smoothies.

When you add yogurt, milk, or ice cream to the pulp you have a source of protein in your deliciously thick drink. As you are using the whole fruit or vegetable you benefit from consuming the fiber too.

JUST
ADD WATER

Healthy bodies need lots of water, so keep a glass with you throughout the day

Water may not be listed as an essential nutrient but without it you cannot function. Two-thirds of your body is water and all the chemical reactions take place because of it. It is important, then, to keep drinking.

You will already be dehydrated when you're thirsty, so aim to drink at least four pints a day. This does seem a lot, so it's good to know that tasty juices count in your quota. Being mostly water, raw juice cleanses and nurtures your system while also supplying vital nutrients.

You would have to eat four or five cups of chopped carrots to equal the nutrients in one cup of juice. That's a lot of chewing!

IT'S GOOD FOR YOU

Beyond making you feel great, juices can help relieve certain complaints

Drinking juice gives the body an instant hit of vitamins, minerals, enzymes, carbohydrates, chlorophyll, and loads of other phytonutrients (which are nutrients from plants) and these all boost your health, giving you more energy, supporting the body's natural cleansing processes, and lowering your susceptibility to coughs and colds.

11

Juices are also full of antioxidants. These attack oxygen molecules, known as free radicals, which damage healthy blood cells and can cause hardening of the arteries. Antioxidants include vitamins A, C, and E, and are believed to help guard against cancer, heart disease, and the effects of aging. They are essential to a younger-looking skin. Also present in many fruit and vegetables is folic acid—great for strong hair and nails.

Good health should not be defined as the absence of disease. Instead it should be seen as a positive, dynamic condition. The best way to achieve that is to consume the right quantities of fresh food.

If you make your drinks in a blender rather than a juicer you will retain the original fiber of the food. This is needed for efficient digestion. If not, make sure you support your juice drinks with a well-balanced diet.

When juicing you must still eat from other food groups (grains, dairy, and pulses) and you shouldn't try to diet by cutting out fat completely—some vitamins need fat to work. You should also ensure that you drink a broad range of fruit and vegetable juices to get a variety of vitamins and minerals.

Apart from taking preventative action by drinking juice for the sake of your health, your intake of particular kinds of fruit and vegetables may help in combating the effects of certain common complaints, and some have been listed here for reference.

If you are following a special diet or are under medical supervision, are diabetic, or suffer from hypoglycemia or gout, consult your doctor before making any drastic changes to your diet.

13

ACNE

Blemishes are usually caused by hormonal imbalance or a diet high in sugar and low in fiber. When the body is not eliminating waste properly, the pores become blocked. Drink plenty of water, cut out junk food, eat vegetables rich in fiber, and try carrot juice or green juices.

CELLULITE

The dimpled skin on certain areas of women's bodies is usually a sign that the lymphatic system isn't taking the toxins out of the body efficiently. Skin brushing and regular exercise will help. You should cut out convenience foods, coffee, and tea. Juices rich in bioflavonoids will help —such as sweet peppers, tomatoes, cabbage, parsley, and citrus fruits.

COMMON COLD

At the sign of the first symptom, drink juices containing onion or garlic, as they can stop the infection. Carrot and apple are good too.

CRAMP

This may be caused by a lack of minerals such as potassium and magnesium, so take blackcurrant, passion fruit, and melon. Banana is also good.

DETOXIFICATION

Most juices are deeply cleansing but you can also embark on a juice fast, replacing food with juices. If you wish to try this, follow an established program and seek advice from your doctor before going ahead.

DIGESTION

Cabbage juice is beneficial and, will taste better if mixed with pineapple! Ginger is also good and bananas have been found to protect the stomach from excess acid.

ECZEMA AND PSORIASIS

These skin problems have a variety of causes. If triggered by stress or fatigue, take plenty of rest and drink pure, cleansing juices.

FATIGUE

This is often due to lack of
iron, particularly in women,
so take spinach or any of
the green leafy vegetables
as a juice. Eat plenty of raw
foods and give it all time
to work—don't expect to
see changes overnight!

HANGOVER

To combat the dehydration
and nausea, fruit juice is
recommended but watermelon
might be kinder on a delicate
stomach. Carrot and apple are

17

good for rebalancing the body and, if you take beets, you will help repair any damage to your liver and kidneys.

HEADACHE

This can be caused by any number of factors including stress, poor diet, or tiredness. If this is a recurring problem consult your doctor. You might like to try the juice from peppers, sweet potato, and carrots.

INSOMNIA

Take up some form of relaxation technique, cut out coffee and alcohol, eat your biggest meal at lunchtime and try lettuce-based juices half an hour before going to bed.

NAUSEA

Ginger is extremely calming as a tea or when mixed in juices.

PMS

Go for green juices which are rich in magnesium, B6, and the B-complex. To alleviate water retention, try watermelon, grape, cucumber, and dandelion.

SKIN

Regularly drinking cleansing, antioxidant juices will benefit your appearance as much as your internal health, and the results show in your skin very quickly. You should ensure you drink plenty of water and cut down on alcohol, tea, and coffee.

STRESS

Certain nutrients are good at strengthening your body's ability to handle stress: pantothenic acid, which occurs in green, leafy vegetables; potassium found in bananas, parsley, and spinach; zinc in carrots and ginger; and magnesium in green vegetables.

When starting out making juices, drink carefully. Your body will need to adjust to this injection of goodness, so increase your intake gradually.

CHANGE YOUR LIFE

You are more likely to keep to good drinking habits if you introduce gradual changes

So you know that you should be consuming five portions of fruit and vegetables a day, as well as drinking those eight glasses of water, but do you do it? You really will feel better if you follow this healthy drinking advice, so here are a few tips to making that change to your daily diet.

First things first: as soon as you get up, make yourself a glass of hot water adding a slice of lemon and a spoonful of honey to taste. This helps to cleanse the system.

Replace your first cup of coffee with an invigorating, vitamin-packed juice or smoothie. Then drink a glass of water with every meal throughout the day. If you don't like the taste, add a splash of fruit juice or a slice of lemon or lime.

If you work in an office, keep a supply of fresh water on your desk. By repeatedly filling your glass from a 67.6 fl. oz bottle you will see how quickly you are reaching your quota. However, bottled water isn't necessarily best. Water from the faucet is normally fine, or you might like to drink filtered water—whatever suits you. Just keep drinking.

Cut down on tea and coffee, and sugary, carbonated drinks, by replacing them with juices, and herbal or fruit teas. There is a vast selection of these teas available so make sure you find one you enjoy.

It's not forbidden to drink tea or coffee, and research often indicates that they can benefit

your health in some ways, but remember that they are stimulants and are diuretic which means that you end up losing more water than you gain.

If you exercise, and the current advice is thirty minutes of moderate exercise at least five times a week, you will need to drink more water to replace fluids lost through perspiration. Remember to keep a water bottle handy at all times and keep sipping!

Now what about alcohol? Just make sure you keep within the daily guideline of 2-3 units for women and 3-4 units for men. Don't drink on an empty stomach, and drink a glass of water for every one of alcohol. The antioxidants in fresh juices will help fight the bad effects of alcohol, but be kind to yourself and don't overdo it!

At bedtime, green tea makes a good relaxing drink, or hot milk and honey works well. Have some water by the bedside too!

MAKING YOUR OWN DRINKS

The time you take whizzing up these concoctions is nothing at all, and they taste fantastic

The juice you make at home and drink immediately will give you better nutritional value than any shop-bought variety. Don't be surprised if it looks different, being particularly bright—or murky—in color, thicker in consistency or with a froth on top. Just stir and drink.

Most fruit and vegetables can be juiced—even the most solid root vegetables can make surprisingly good juice. You can also add fresh herbs and spices to your concoctions for a whole new slant on nutrients and flavors. Fresh ginger is particularly good and acts as a stimulant as well as warming the body.

All of the recipes included in this book make single servings. Simply add water or increase the quantities for more juice.

GOLDEN RULES

If your ingredients are pulpy, like carrots or celery, they will need a juicer. Melon or peach, on the other hand, will produce a lovely, smooth drink by being blended.

Choose fruits which are not quite ripe as these will give you the most juice and the best taste.

Be wary of drinking strong juices by themselves. Add water or blend with cucumber. Always dilute juices with water for young children.

Always try to buy organic produce, so that you can use the whole fruit or vegetable. Always scrub fruit or vegetables, and peel non-organic produce.

Buy the best. The better the condition of the raw ingredients, the better the nutritional value. Try to buy in season and when the fruit is ripe, but not overripe. Vary juices so that you consume a wide range of fruit and vegetables.

As soon as you cut into the fruit and vegetables they become exposed to the air and oxidization takes place. At this time nutrients are lost, so only prepare your ingredients when you are ready. In addition you might like to pour the juice into a container which holds a squeeze of lemon juice. It's best to drink your juice immediately after you've made it to avoid oxidization at this stage. Although you can store juices in a vacuum flask, or screw-topped glass bottle in a fridge, it's best to make juice as you need it.

You can also freeze juices, but mixes often separate and don't work well so it's better to freeze single fruit or vegetable juices.

GETTING THE EQUIPMENT

The drinks included here can be made using a variety of methods, from simply squeezing, to juicing and blending. A lemon-squeezer is sufficient for extracting the juice from citrus fruit. You might like to progress to a citrus press if you juice this type of fruit frequently since they are more labor saving.

The centrifugal juicer is the most widely available and cheapest style of machine. Fruit and vegetables are fed into a rapidly spinning grater which separates the pulp from the juice.

The masticating juicer mashes the fruit or vegetable and pushes it with great force through a mesh wire, producing a great quantity of juice.

When juicing dense root vegetables, fibrous green herbs and vegetables, feed only small quantities into the juicer at a time and alternate them with a vegetable which juices easily.

The hydraulic press extracts juice by exerting tremendous force and filters out the juice through a mesh or muslin. It is efficient but expensive.

A food processor or blender works by puréeing ingredients and is used to make thicker, smoothie-style drinks.

Cleaning the juicer is probably the bit that puts people off. However, as long as you choose a juicer which dismantles easily, it is simply a question of running the parts under the hot faucet immediately after you have used it. Don't leave it to stand on the kitchen worktop for hours, as you will have a terrible job getting rid of the stuff that has dried on. After heavy usage, you might need to soak the parts in a mild solution of vinegar and water.

The pulp remaining after you have extracted the juice can be used in soups, or even breads and cakes. Alternatively, add it to a compost heap so that your garden benefits too.

ENERGY BOOST
DRINKS

Fatigue and exhaustion are common reasons why people seek a doctor but there's rarely a medical condition behind it.

One solution is to learn to eat better. You should avoid high sugar and refined carbohydrate foods. These give you an instant but short-lived high at the same time as increasing your risk of diabetes, obesity, and heart disease. Instead, try these invigorating drinks which combine slow- and quick-release energy. They will reduce the risk of diabetes and help boost your vitality and overall health.

1 kiwi fruit
1 apple
1 carrot

KIWI KICK

This is a sweet drink which is energy-giving, good for your skin and will help fight off infection.

MAKE IT: top and tail the carrot. Remove the stalk of the apple. Add the kiwi (with or without the peel, although it can taste bitter), juice or blend. Experiment with different apples.

1 mango
$\frac{1}{2}$ small pineapple
1 small banana
5 tbsp natural yogurt
6 tbsp pineapple juice

TROPICAL MANGO

With a fantastic flavor, mangoes are high in betacarotene and a good source of vitamins A, C, and E. There's folic acid too!

MAKE IT: put all the ingredients in the blender for this creamy, delicious drink.

Also, try blending mangoes on their own with yogurt—they're made for each other!

4 tomatoes
1 carrot
½ lemon
a handful of basil

POWERING
THROUGH

Containing lycopene, protecting against heart disease, this juice will also reinvigorate both tired muscles and minds.

MAKE IT: trim the ingredients, then juice or blend together. You could also add an extra bite with some black pepper and a little Worcestershire sauce to taste.

39

a handful of parsley

3 carrots

1 kiwi fruit, peeled

1 apple

PARSLEY
PASSION

Good for women with fluid retention as its gentle stimulants will get rid of excess fluid. Parsley is also good as a breath freshener!

MAKE IT: trim the ingredients, then juice or blend. A great way to start the day, this drink will give you extra strength to fight off infection and will keep skin and eyes healthy.

1 banana
$\frac{1}{2}$ pear
$\frac{1}{2}$ orange
4 tbsp apple juice

TOP BANANA

Bananas can't go through the juicer so try blending to give a lovely thickness to drinks.

MAKE IT: combine all in a blender. Banana is a great fast food. It's full of fiber, high in calories, boosts potassium and vitamin B and, with serotonin, it keeps you happy!

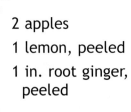

2 apples
1 lemon, peeled
1 in. root ginger,
  peeled

THE BIG APPLE

Experiment with different types of apples as you'll find their flavors are more pronounced when juiced.

MAKE IT: trim the fruit and finely cut the ginger, then juice or blend. This is a fantastic juice with a real kick. It's good as a morning pick-me-up and is sure to put a spring in your step!

44

6 grapes

1 pear

1 apple

1 slice pineapple,
 peeled

PEARING UP

The smell from the pears alone is enough
to rid you of any lethargy in this wonderfully,
sweet and creamy drink.

MAKE IT: trim
ingredients, then juice.
Soluble fiber in the
apples and pears, and
sugars in the grapes
and pineapple, provide
an instant energy boost
that aids digestion.

½ red pepper, deseeded

½ yellow pepper, deseeded

2 medium carrots

PICK A PEPPER

Add a few lettuce leaves to make a mild diuretic and laxative, or add a small beet to act against anemia.

MAKE IT: trim ingredients. Juice or blend. A surprisingly sweet-tasting juice, packed with antioxidants, it is good for your skin, your immune system and gives an energy boost.

CLEANSING DRINKS

Modern living, with all its pollution, central heating, and chemically-treated and processed food, clogs up our system. It's good then to have a clear out, and cleansing drinks are a tasty, easy way to do it.

These natural, pure ingredients have their own specific properties to aid the digestive process. They can rescue you from spots, fluid retention, a general bloated feeling, or lethargy. Once you've felt the benefits you might go on to try a full detox plan.

51

3 apples
a handful of spinach

SPIN DOCTOR

Mixing apple and spinach cleanses the digestive system and quickly improves elimination. This is surprisingly tasty!

MAKE IT: trim the ingredients, then juice or blend. Spinach is good to strengthen bones, teeth, and gums. It regulates blood pressure and acts as a natural laxative.

a small bunch of mint
honey to taste
boiling water

MINT TEA

A refreshing, light drink that's good
for digestion.

MAKE IT: pour water
over the mint leaves,
steep for five minutes.
Stir in the honey.

As an alternative, cool,
then top up with
pineapple juice and
add ice.

½ cucumber
1 apple

COOL CLEANSER

Adjust the ingredients to suit your taste because this is a simple, but effective, cooling drink!

MAKE IT: trim the ingredients, then juice or blend. A refreshing, light drink. Cucumber is also good to add to other juices if you want to dilute the flavor of them slightly.

2 beets
2 apples
3 sticks of celery

RED BLOODED

Beets are fantastic for building up the blood. This drink combines beets and fruit and is packed with vitamin C and minerals.

MAKE IT: trim the ingredients, then juice or blend. Beet juice is good to combat kidney stones, gall bladder and liver problems, and for anemia. It is definitely worth trying!

59

$^1/_2$ melon, with skin

$^1/_2$ small pineapple,
   peeled

a small bunch of mint

MELON MINT

Enjoy the aroma of this frothy, sweet drink.
Melon is great as a cleansing ingredient and
pineapple is full of minerals.

MAKE IT: trim the
ingredients, then juice
or blend. Melon has a
high water content so
goes through the body
at great speed! It
removes bloating and
puffiness as it goes.

½ red pepper, deseeded
3 carrots
a handful of spinach
a handful of parsley

PURIFYING PEPPER

An unusual color, this drink is good for cleansing and replenishing nutrients. Try adding a small beet.

MAKE IT: trim ingredients. Juice or blend. Parsley is a diuretic and stimulates the kidneys. Carrot and red pepper work on the large bowel. Spinach purifies the blood.

63

2 oz prunes, pitted

8 fl. oz cup of water

4 fl. oz cup of apple juice

PRUNE AND
APPLE SMOOTHIE

Prunes are good for fiber, iron, potassium, and vitamin B6. All dried fruits make great smoothies —try blending apricots or dates.

MAKE IT: in a saucepan, bring the prunes to the boil in the water, then cover and simmer for 10 minutes. Allow to cool, then blend with the apple juice. Add black pepper to taste.

a handful of watercress
2 apples
1 kiwi

WATERFALL

Watercress is one of the most healing and protective juices. It is an excellent detoxifier and blood purifier.

MAKE IT: trim the ingredients, then juice or blend. Watercress has a very strong taste. It doesn't produce much juice but it is powerful. It should only form $\frac{1}{6}$ of any juice mixture.

QUICK FIX DRINKS

If it's too late for you to take the preventative route, or you need an extra boost of energy to cope with illness or new demands of the day, what better answer than to whiz up a refreshing and invigorating drink!

As the juice is so readily absorbed by the body, you will enjoy the benefits of the ingredients immediately. Of course certain fruits and vegetables are ideal for certain complaints.

Don't struggle through the day, make yourself a juice!

68

2 carrots
1 orange

CARROT TOP

You're sure to have these ingredients in the house and they make a powerful and tasty combination

MAKE IT: top and tail the carrot. Remove the skin and pith from the orange. Juice. This blast of vitamin C, betacarotene, folic acid, and numerous minerals gives an energy boost which builds your immunity.

2 oranges
1 in. root ginger
sparkling water

JUST THE TONIC

A great introduction to juicing and a refreshing drink at any time.

MAKE IT: juice the ginger and orange and top up with the mineral water.

Orange may seem run-of-the-mill, but nothing can beat the taste of freshly-squeezed juice.

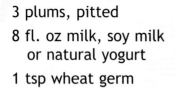

3 plums, pitted

8 fl. oz milk, soy milk
   or natural yogurt

1 tsp wheat germ

PLUM SHAKE

A great introduction to juicing and a refreshing drink at any time.

MAKE IT: place all the ingredients in a blender. Plums are a highly antioxidant fruit and with their high iron content, they can help combat anemia and strengthen the blood.

2 oranges

1 lemon

1 lime

1 grapefruit,
yellow or pink

CITRUS MIX

This is sure to be a favorite drink. Clean, tangy, great in the morning, it is good for digestion and to combat a hangover.

MAKE IT: juice all the ingredients. If you are on any medication, consult your doctor before drinking large amounts of grapefruit juice.

4 tomatoes
1 sweet potato
1 in. root ginger
2 sticks of celery

WAKE-UP CALL

A powerful drink that will kick you into action for the day. It is a rehydrating juice and powerful antioxidant.

MAKE IT: trim the ingredients, then juice or blend. Replace the ginger and sweet potato with carrots, cucumber and half a beet. Or keep it simple with just tomatoes and celery.

1 small raw beet
2 carrots
2 oranges

BEET TREAT

Beets are one of the best juices for cleansing and bolstering blood.

MAKE IT: top and tail the carrots and scrub the beet. Remove the peel and pith of the orange, then juice.

Apples are an alternative to oranges. You'll find there are quite a number of things you can mix with beets.

1 lemon
1 tsp honey
water

GRANNY'S COLD CURE

A traditional, soothing drink to combat a chill, sore throat or to take when feeling under the weather.

MAKE IT: squeeze the lemon. Add the honey. Pour on boiling water and drink.

A time-honored way to deal with the onset of a cold. If you've run out of lemons, try an orange.

1 large sweet potato
1 leek
2 carrots
2 sticks of celery

CLEAR YOUR HEAD

A good antioxidant cocktail that will help relieve headaches. The juice is also cleansing, energizing and said to be beneficial for ulcers.

MAKE IT: trim the ingredients, then juice or blend. This is a powerful, earthy drink which has a real kick from the leek. Root vegetables are a good source of B-complex vitamins.

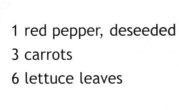

1 red pepper, deseeded
3 carrots
6 lettuce leaves

TRAFFIC LIGHT

Lettuce contains a lot of water and is highly diuretic. It has calming properties that make it good as a late-night drink to aid sleep.

MAKE IT: clean and trim the ingredients, then juice or blend. Lettuce is a strong, green juice that needs to be diluted with other sweeter flavors. You could try it with apple or parsley.

IMMUNITY DRINKS

If you have a tendency to catch every cold that's going and regularly suffer from throat or bladder infections, your immune system might need a boost.

Regularly drinking fresh juices, healthy drinks and smoothies is sure to help but the following juice mixes are particularly good.

1 small pineapple
6 sage leaves
¹/₂ cucumber
3 carrots

THROAT SOOTHER

A tasty, sweet drink which will fight mouth and throat infections.

MAKE IT: clean and trim ingredients, then juice or blend. Try different herbs and spices with your drinks as they can make quite a difference to the other flavors. Sage is a powerful antiseptic and you can feel it doing you good!

$^1/_2$ pineapple
$^1/_4$ white cabbage

SWEET CABBAGE

Cabbage juice is too strong to drink on its own but is a powerful antioxidant, building up immunity from diseases and cleansing.

MAKE IT: trim the ingredients, then juice or blend. You could add 1 in. of root ginger and fresh mint.

Different types of cabbage will produce different types of juice and benefits. White is the sweetest.

1 head of broccoli
2 carrots

SPROUTING
HEALTH

Broccoli is a wonder juice. It is a deep cleanser giving you great skin and bright eyes plus tremendous health benefits.

MAKE IT: trim the ingredients, then juice or blend. You can add a red pepper if you wish. Broccoli is a little bitter so should always be mixed with something sweeter like carrot or beets.

3 carrots
a bunch of watercress
a handful of spinach

BRIGHT EYES

There was truth in the old wives' tale that carrots help you see in the dark. Carotenoids are good for eye health and protection.

MAKE IT: trim the ingredients, then juice or blend. Spinach and watercress both cleanse the body. Don't overdo it with the spinach and choose small, bright green leaves.

½ yellow melon,
   deseeded and sliced

3 carrots

½-1 clove of garlic

1 in. root ginger

ALL ROUNDER

A smooth, tasty drink with a kick as the ginger
and garlic set in! Your friends will know you've
taken this drink!

MAKE IT: trim the ingredients, then juice or blend. Garlic and ginger are good for the heart and circulation, and melon, with its high vitamin C, is good for the immune system.

2 carrots

2 apples

COLD BUSTER

This combination is one of the best immune system boosters and detoxifiers and is great for your skin.

MAKE IT: trim the ingredients, then juice. Red apples will give a sweeter flavor. This is a good staple on which to experiment in combining flavors. Spice this drink up with half a lime, or 1 in. of root ginger.

1/2 melon
1/2 cucumber
1/4 white cabbage
a bunch of parsley

GREEN DREAM

Great for the skin and as a detox, this drink also aids digestion.

MAKE IT: trim the ingredients, then juice or blend. This is a refreshing, light drink which, as a diuretic, will help eliminate excess fluids from the body.

$^1/_2$ pineapple

a bunch of mint

So to Sleep

Particularly good at night to settle the stomach and help you to sleep. Or it would make a nice, cooling summer drink with ice.

MAKE IT: trim the ingredients then blend or juice. Pineapple is also good with lime, orange and ginger, apples, or watermelon.

BUILD-UP
DRINKS

More substantial drinks, adding protein to the vitamin-fueled juices, can be beneficial in supporting an exercise program, or if you need boosting after illness, for example.

Some fruits are naturally life-enhancing—banana, in particular, makes a great fast food and the drinks included here will be quicker to make than a sandwich!

1 large banana
1 tbsp peanut butter
1 tbsp crème fraîche
a pinch of cinnamon

BANANA SMOOTHIE

The riper the banana, the deeper the flavor—you can even get away with using brown bananas here.

MAKE IT: blend until smooth. You could also try banana with soy milk and ground almonds, or with half fat milk and avocado.

109

7 oz canned peaches

4 fl. oz soy milk or
 natural yogurt

sunflower or sesame
 seeds or chopped nuts

STORE-CUPBOARD
REMEDY

If you need a pick-me-up but haven't got fresh
fruit to hand, use canned. However, make sure it
is in natural juice or water, not syrup.

MAKE IT: blend all the ingredients together. This is a delicious, creamy drink to whiz up when the fruit bowl is empty!

$^1/_2$ mango

1 medium orange

4 fl. oz natural yogurt

FRUITY FLING

Mango is high in antioxidants and is believed to counteract some cancers. It is good for the kidneys and in cleansing the blood.

MAKE IT: juice the fruit, then blend with the yogurt for a delicious drink. Make sure your mango is ripe and you will be guaranteed a heavenly, smooth drink which boasts the protein and cultures of the yogurt.

113

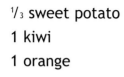

1/3 sweet potato
1 kiwi
1 orange

SMASHER

A sweet, refreshing drink which will give you an energy boost.

MAKE IT: scrub the sweet potato, remove the peel and pith from orange and kiwi. Juice.

Sweet potatoes are easier to digest and higher in fiber than regular potatoes.

114

¹/₄ pineapple
1 small orange
1 small banana
1 tsp honey
4 fl. oz natural yogurt

TROPICAL
TANTALIZER

You could also add coconut milk for a truly tropical taste.

MAKE IT: cut off the top and bottom of the pineapple and remove the skin, removing all the eyes.

Juice the orange. Blend the orange and pineapple together with all the other ingredients.

117

- 1 kiwi
- 2 sprigs of mint
- 2 tsp lemon juice
- 1 tsp honey
- 5 fl. oz grapefruit juice
- 2 tbsp protein powder

ZEST FOR LIFE

Kiwi has three times the vitamin C of citrus fruit and also has an enzyme which helps the digestive system break down protein.

MAKE IT: juice the kiwi with the mint and blend with lemon juice, honey and half the grapefruit juice. Finally, add the protein powder —a supplement sold in health food stores.

9 oz strawberries
2 oranges

ROSY GLOW

It does seem a shame to juice a strawberry but this is a great-tasting drink. You could also add grapefruit.

MAKE IT: remove the peel and pith from the oranges, then juice with the strawberries.

The strawberry is one of the richest sources of vitamin C and also contains calcium.

TOP TIPS

Before you experiment with your own flavors, here are some points to remember

The recipes included in this book are merely guides to get you going as you will find an almost limitless range of combinations. You can turn the juices into smoothies or shakes by adding milk or yogurt, and can blend instead of juice in many cases.

Don't forget to try your favorite fruit and vegetables on their own—orange juice may seem boring after all the varieties we've listed but it is a different drink altogether when freshly squeezed at home.

Different varieties of apples give distinct flavors so juice to find your favorite.

You can introduce other ingredients such as ground nuts and seeds, to your drinks. Spirulina is a form of chlorophyll which is believed to halt the signs of aging. It is a good addition in juices but may spoil the color. Wheatgrass is also rich in chlorophyll and boosts immunity. Seaweeds and powdered cereal grasses stirred into the juice are also worth trying.

Citrus juices are highly acidic and are best diluted, either with other juices or water.

There is a general rule that you shouldn't mix vegetables and fruit in the same juice, except carrots and apples which blend well with almost anything. There are exceptions.

Generally fruit is good for detoxifying your body and vegetables are good at adding the nutritional foundation for the reactions in the body.

Avoid too many strong-tasting vegetables in one juice.

If using strong or bitter-tasting vegetables, dilute and sweeten them with cucumber and carrot. The darker the juice, the more it needs to be diluted.

If you want to use canned fruit, make sure it is in natural juice or water, not syrup.

Dried fruits like apricots, prunes, and dates are a concentrated source of sugars, vitamins, and minerals. Soak them overnight to make them easier to purée.

Any seeds or nuts included in your drinks should be blended until completely smooth.

To prevent juices going brown as they oxidize and losing nutrients, pour them into a glass containing a little lemon juice—or drink immediately!

When selecting fruit for smoothies, make sure they are at their ripest for the best taste.

You should wash all your fresh ingredients well, but don't soak as this will weaken their nutritional value.

Most herbs and spices make tasty teas which are good for you, so try growing a ready supply in your garden.

For thicker smoothies use yogurt. Runnier drinks can be made with milk, and soy milk is a non-dairy alternative.

If you have to peel your ingredients, keep the peel as thin as possible because many of the nutrients are stored in this outer layer.

Thick juices and smoothies can also be frozen on sticks or you can blend some crushed ice cubes with the ingredients to make a refreshingly cool drink.

You'll have found that when you make juicing part of your daily routine, it is quick and straightforward, rewarded by a great-tasting drink which is also an easy and effective way of taking control of your diet and health.

LAST WORDS

We hope that by now you will be convinced that juicing is easy, fun, and delicious

Combine juicing with a balanced diet and at least thirty minutes of moderate exercise five days a week, and it shouldn't be long before you start to notice the difference. So, don't be afraid to spread the good news to friends and family—when you feel this good it would be wrong not to share it!

126

INDEX